AT HOME

ALFREDO PAREDES
AT HOME

FOREWORD BY RALPH LAUREN

WRITTEN WITH BRAD GOLDFARB

RIZZOLI NEW YORK
New York Paris London Milan

FOR MY THREE LOVES—
BRAD, CAROLINA, AND SEBASTIAN

FEELING
Bruce Weber
LITTLE BEAR PRESS

CONTENTS

FOREWORD

In 1986, I was building my dream of a store on Madison Avenue. I chose a beautiful old mansion on the corner of Seventy-Second Street. Alfredo had just joined our creative team at age twenty-three, and that's when I met and began working with him. He told me he had grown up in Miami, part of a large family—the first generation of Cuban Americans in exile. He shared with me that he was "steeped in Ralph Lauren as a kid." When he asked his mother for a Polo shirt, though, she told him, "No, it's too expensive." And so he had to wait until he was older and could get a job to buy one for himself. (He says he eventually bought twelve.)

Alfredo started by arranging visual displays on the first and second floors of the Mansion and changing windows late at night. Eventually, I took him under my wing because I saw not just his talent, but his passion and love for creating and storytelling. I guess I saw a little of myself in him when I first started out. It was only a few years later that I asked him to take over our store development, creative services, and eventually our Home Collection. I believed in him, and he ran with all these for thirty-three years. From Madison Avenue to Boulevard Saint-Germain, to Bond Street and Dubai, to Moscow, to the Polo Bar and Ralph's Coffee, to our fiftieth anniversary event in Central Park, he steered these and so much more.

As much as he devoted himself to working, Alfredo never forgot about living, which is what this beautiful book celebrates: the very personal homes he has created and lived in with his husband, Brad, and eventually their young daughter, Carolina, and son, Sebastian.

I am honored to welcome you in.

—Ralph Lauren

INTRODUCTION

When talking about my professional background and especially the years I spent writing about design, people will sometimes ask me if I studied art history or architecture. The answer, I must confess, is no–I was a French and English lit major. But I'm equally quick to add that I've lived with Alfredo Paredes for the past thirty-five years, and that has been its own education. This usually gets half a laugh and a knowing nod because, of course, what better way to learn the language and basic history of design—not to mention a general who's who and what's what of the interior design profession—than at the right hand of one of the industry's best?

Let's just acknowledge up front that I'm a little biased. Maybe more than a little. In addition to being my partner in all things for over thirty years, Alfredo has been my husband for the past decade, so there's no question—where this man's formidable talents are concerned, I'll be first in line to heap on the accolades.

But they're also deserved.

Aside from watching Alfredo grow through his long career at Ralph Lauren, during which his responsibilities and influence evolved and expanded exponentially, I've also been by his side through the design of all eight of our shared homes (four are featured here). In other words, I've seen up-close what so many who have worked with Alfredo know—a gifted musician might be said to have a perfect ear, but as a family member aptly put it after a first visit to our home in the early 1990s, Alfredo has perfect visual pitch.

It's something I noticed early on in our relationship, long before I had a clear understanding of what Alfredo actually did during the workday. I grew up in homes where things were static—the ashtray went here, the framed family photo went there, and rarely, if ever, did things budge from their designated spot or position. But Alfredo would return to our home after a short work trip somewhere, and before it seemed he'd even put down his bags, a lamp would be shifted, a chair repositioned, a stack of books realigned just so and, suddenly, the space would sing anew. Those slight adjustments would alter the whole mood in the room, making it feel warmer and more welcoming; inanimate objects seemed somehow refreshed. The transformation would leave me speechless, as if I'd witnessed some sort of magic trick.

This talent is something Ralph Lauren and his team quickly picked up on when

THE ART OF JAZZ
ESSAYS ON THE NATURE AND DEVELOPMENT OF JAZZ
EDITED BY MARTIN T. WILLIAMS
SOLARIUM
EL EDISON
JOAN MIRÓ
l'été
Une femme brûlée par les
flammes du soleil attrape un papillon qui s'
envole poussé par le souffle d'une fourmi se
réposant à l'ombre arc-en-ciel
du ventre de la femme devant la mer
les aiguilles de ses seins tournées vers
les vagues qui envoient un sourire blanc
rose au Croissant
de la lune
3495

they hired Alfredo in 1986, just a year out of art school but already making a name for himself in Washington, DC. At the time he was working in visual display for everyone from Britches of Georgetown to Uzzolo on Dupont Circle–then the city's hippest home décor store, where Alfredo created a spur-of-the-moment, no-budget installation featuring a multitude of Pyrex vases filled with oranges and lemons bought at the corner deli. It was a splashy move for DC in the mid-eighties, one that got him mentioned in the paper.

At that time, the Rhinelander Mansion at Seventy-Second Street and Madison Avenue in New York City was being converted into the first stand-alone Ralph Lauren store; following the suggestion of Stephen Brady, an early mentor of Alfredo's and a recent Ralph Lauren hire himself, Alfredo was brought on as part of the visual display team. In this new role, he was part of the group responsible for the look of the store's interior and its all-important window displays. Under the guidance of the legendary Jeff Walker, Alfredo quickly distinguished himself with his creativity, his visual finesse, and his ability to both channel Mr. Lauren's vision and to expand it, creating immersive worlds inspired by those glamorous, fabulous clothes. The store itself, brimming with antique rugs, oil portraits, and miles of mahogany woodwork, was big news when it opened, offering an early taste of the designer's now-famous aesthetic. But the eight large-scale windows fronting Madison Avenue became the best, most direct advertisement for the brand. It was there that Alfredo initially made his mark.

Whether they were scenes depicting an ostensibly aristocratic summer activity, such as a croquet party, first-class travel, or any other aspirational pursuit, what those early windows communicated was a type of glamour typically associated with movies of the 1930s and '40s. Ralph Lauren the man has, of course, long acknowledged the importance of film as an inspiration—an affinity that Alfredo shares as well and a factor that provided a deep creative connection and the foundation for a common language between them.

Ask Alfredo, and he'll tell you that his design education began as a kid watching episodes of the *Beverly Hillbillies* and *Gilligan's Island*. He first revealed this to me early in our relationship, and the confession left me a bit baffled given that neither show offered much in the way of set design or art direction. But over time I came to realize that was the point: For Alfredo, a mere glimpse of a Gothic column or a Polynesian-style grass hut at the edge or rear of a shot offered just enough for him to imagine an entire world. Those small visual suggestions were all he needed. He used the same technique often at Ralph Lauren. Even the smallest details in his window displays—a botanical print tacked to a wall, a string of pearls pooling around a highball glass, a vintage typewriter and a waste bin half filled with balled-up paper—could similarly transport us into the lives of the seemingly exciting, enviable, glamorous people wearing Lauren's fabulous clothes. Staring into those windows was mesmerizing—and effective. Want that life? Buy the shirt.

With this singular aim to entice by storytelling, Alfredo and his talented cohorts at Ralph Lauren could create rooms and environments that acted on your brain almost subconsciously, so whether it was a showroom for the Home Collection depicting a perfectly appointed Parisian garret or windows offering an idealized version of a western rancher's homestead, if only for a moment you'd find yourself saying, "Yes! This is exactly how I want to live." Again, a kind of magic.

Years ago, when we had a weekend home in East Hampton, I used to joke that I could always tell if Alfredo and his crew had recently visited the Ralph Lauren store there because when I'd enter, I'd suddenly want to buy . . . everything. While many of the clothes were indeed terrific, it was the entire experience of the immersive environment that was so compelling. I'd often leave having handed over my credit card for an item or two, but really it was the whole experience I wanted. The clothes, the props, the vintage items (also for sale), and the way they coalesced conjured a powerful emotional response.

In time, Alfredo's role grew to encompass oversight of the company's visual display teams, store development, and the brand's Home Collection Design Studio. This progression from dreaming up environments in which to show the clothes to creating home products inspired by the clothes themselves was in many ways a natural one. During his thirty-plus years with the company, Alfredo worked closely with Mr. Lauren on this, often intuiting or extrapolating what he was after from a few simple words or even the style of a single item of clothing—a creative process very much in sync with how the designer himself works and sees the world. So the stripe on an Oxford shirt became inspiration for a bedding collection, an embroidered pheasant on a pair of velvet slippers evolved into a throw pillow. Alfredo's job was to provide context for the individual pieces, to imagine an environment in which they could live as Mr. Lauren had imagined. Their shared visual language brought those worlds to life in a way that felt hip and modern even as it nodded to a glamorized past.

This acknowledgment of our need for a little fantasy and desire continues today in Alfredo's work with his current roster of clients. Their dialogue is always, on some level, about their forward-looking vision of themselves and how they hope to live in a given space. Be it a seaside villa on the Baja California Peninsula, a spacious family home in the country reimagined for empty nesters eager to welcome grandchildren, or the renovation of a venerable club built early in the last century and looking to reclaim its luster, on some level the question always comes down to, "What movie do you see yourself starring in here?" Every project has the potential to tell a story, and when that story aligns with the client's vision of themselves or the space, well, let's just say everyone lives happily ever after.

A certain appreciation, reverence even, for the past was very much a part of Alfredo's childhood in Miami, Florida. As a first-generation American of Cuban descent, and the first born in his family unit, Alfredo was weaned on stories of the Havana Yacht Club and debutante parties at the presidential palace—the family's personal paradise lost. The one time I met his grandmother, a kind of Auntie Mame figure as flamboyant as she was warm, she told me how she'd smuggled her not-inconsiderable collection of jewelry out of Cuba by hiding it in her hair—teased and sprayed into a beehive. This ingenuity ultimately supported the family in their early years as immigrants, as she was compelled to sell the jewelry off for pennies on the dollar. For a creative kid whose idea of fun when his parents were out was to corral his three siblings into moving all the furniture onto the lawn so he could redecorate the house, stories like these were a powerful influence.

Alfredo came of age in the bohemian culture of 1970s Miami, with its mix of hippie cool and Latin American swagger, and this too left a mark. I've felt these influences in all the homes we've shared over the years—evident here in his liberal use of potted plants of all shapes and sizes, there as abundant natural wood and rustic woven textiles. More tellingly, they come through in the general *un*done quality of the spaces and objects he touches. And by that I don't mean unconsidered or unfinished, but rather a confident looseness and dynamism. Alfredo's

WARHOL ON BASQUIAT
TASCHEN
SILVER. SKATE. SEVENTIES.
Hugh Holland
FRANÇOIS HALARD
ALEXANDER McQUEEN: SAVAGE BEAUTY
DAVID YARROW
Interieurs im Portrait
Axel Vervoordt
SCOTT SHRADER THE ART OF OUTDOOR LIVING
TOM FORD

work is the opposite of staid—it's tactile and sexy. Even in the most formal of his spaces, we sense that life is meant to happen there: fun will be had, messes will be made, human dramas will play out with energy and abandon.

A deft use of vintage or antique items, be it furniture or clothing, was a hallmark of Alfredo's work at Ralph Lauren and remains a key component of his design approach today, imbuing a sense of history into the mix. For Alfredo, too much "newness" kills any magic a room might possess, so furniture with nicks and scratches are omnipresent in his work. So too is a mix of high and low, expensive and economical. As he puts it, "too many major pieces cancel each other out."

At times I've jokingly referred to Alfredo as "the house whisperer" for his seeming ability to commune with a long-dead architect's original intent or to intuit what a room or house really wants to be. Among certain of his friends and family Alfredo is known to be almost psychic, often making a move or a change in his personal life at exactly the right moment. In his work it's a talent that helps him to determine what precisely a room needs; this is a skill that serves him well in everything, be it determining where a doorway should be moved or deciding whether to go for that expensive piece of nineteenth-century furniture. When he listens to his instinct, it rarely leads him wrong.

Five years ago, that little voice told him it was time to finally step out from behind the curtain, to strike out on his own. After thirty-three years at a company he had helped to build, working alongside people he adored, this was no small decision. But the voice was persistent, and Alfredo knows better than to ignore his intuition, so he made the leap and Alfredo Paredes Studio was born.

Since then, Alfredo has turned his talents to a variety of residential projects, including a sleek contemporary villa in Miami Beach, a rambling Colonial on the North Shore of Long Island, and a modern ski chalet in Vermont. Each reflects distinct parts of Alfredo's vision while at the same time remaining sensitive to the project's setting and the clients' desires. Alfredo is too engaged with making each place tell its own tale to ever revert to a prescribed design aesthetic. And in keeping with the array of projects he spearheaded during his years at Ralph Lauren, there have been stores, restaurants, and home products including furniture, rugs, textiles, and accessories. In short, he continues to dream, design, and create.

I can't wait to see what comes next.

—Brad Goldfarb

EAST VILLAGE DUPLEX
NEW YORK CITY

I tend to troll online real estate listings pretty compulsively, and one day an East Village duplex popped up in my feed. The agent had given it the sales description of "Palladio in the sky," I guess because of the symmetry of the main room and the gracious way it way opened up to an outdoor space. One of the photos showed a rooftop garden with a view over St. Mark's Church in-the-Bowery, and that really caught my eye. It reminded me of the set from Alfred Hitchcock's *Rope*, with its artist's studio windows and view across Manhattan. The place clearly needed a lot of work but it had three exposures, 13-foot ceilings in the living room, and a giant terrace, albeit covered in tar paper. It was this jewel box of a maisonette and, because it was perched at the top of a building that housed a music school on the bottom three floors, from street level nobody could really tell that it was up there. It reminded me of garret apartments I'd seen in Europe. And there was nothing slick or pretentious about it, which I loved.

I also liked the idea of moving to the East Village—a part of the city I've always been drawn to for its creative spirit. The neighborhood was a magnet for counterculture types when I first moved to New York, and though it's become more gentrified over the years it still retains some of its past grittiness. The only hesitation I had was about how much we were willing to commit financially to realizing this fantasy. I knew the renovations we would want to do would be substantial; did that make sense for an East Village co-op? In the end, it felt enough like a one-of-a-kind property that we went for it.

Aesthetically, I wanted something that felt like it had patina, and for the space to be a transportive surprise in the middle of New York City. At the time I was finding myself drawn to things from Belgium and Holland, so those influences definitely came into play here. Frankly, the whole place reminded me somehow of Amsterdam, in part because of the view of that historic church spire. I also wanted the apartment to feel a little like a Hollywood mogul lived there—perhaps due to the fact that I'd been staying at the Chateau Marmont in Los Angeles a lot at the time and loved the louche spirit of that place.

One major change I knew I wanted to make right from the start was moving the kitchen to one end of the living room, which actually felt too big as originally laid out. And it was clear I needed to move the stair, but that required shifting the position of the front door, an effort in turn hampered by giant support columns. Getting the geometry of all that rearranged was challenging, but once we sorted it out everything else just fell into place.

On the exterior brickwork facing the terrace, there was an arch detail above the double door and each of the four windows. By removing the masonry under those arches and enlarging the window openings we were able to create five matching French doors crowned with semicircular windows, filling the room with light and better integrating the expansive outdoor

PAGE 21: Shifting the front door's position a few feet allowed the floor plan to accommodate a small but gracious entry foyer and a staircase that rises naturally from the hall. French limestone unites the stair, entry-level floor, and outdoor terrace. The wrought-iron railing was produced locally but inspired by a nineteenth-century original from a Florentine office building.

PAGE 22: A wrought-iron pergola installed above the terrace's arched doorways holds boughs of wisteria, providing much-needed screening from midafternoon sunshine. The exterior lanterns are vintage.

RIGHT: Existing semicircle designs in the exterior brickwork inspired us to carve out five arched French doors. A beamed ceiling of reclaimed oak and a wrought-iron lantern from Spain, among the first items purchased for the apartment, gives a sense of history to the space. Rough-out suede was chosen for the George Sherlock sofa and chairs, both for the warmth of its ginger color and for how it would gain character over time. The oak table does double duty as a dining table and a workspace.

RIGHT: Pat Steir's *November Night (1994–95)* commands one end of the living room. The console is a nineteenth-century Belgian worktable. Inset bookcases of bleached oak, a material that appears throughout the apartment, ensures the room feels library-cozy while providing a home for the many art, photography, and design books we've collected over the years. TVs always look better when treated like art; we hung ours on an antique English artist's easel.

living space. We also replaced all the windows in the unit, swapping them out for an iron casement variety. Iron is picked up elsewhere in the interior, too, most notably in the stair railing, which I had fashioned by a local craftsman to emulate one I'd seen and photographed in Florence. Since the living room spills right out onto the terrace, it felt important to choose flooring that could work seamlessly indoors and out to avoid having to change materials. We decided on French limestone, which really enhanced that sense of being somewhere other than New York.

Whenever I'm dealing with a residence that isn't huge, I find a continuity of palette from one room to the next helpful, as it establishes a sense of harmony. Here I stuck to various shades of wood, punctuated by black. I think the only color I added was the chestnut of the rough-out suede in the living room. A big abaca and an English sofa and chairs made it feel very "country house" but at the same time bohemian and modern, thanks to the industrial accents and contemporary black-and-white photography and art on the walls.

The ceilings also presented an opportunity for some bold moves. I knew a big, plain expanse of white sheetrock would be less than inspiring, and given the room's dimensions something enveloping and warm was needed. I really wanted to create a cozy place that would feel great in all seasons, but especially in winter. We decided to emphasize the ceiling and to actually make it a prominent feature of the apartment by adding reclaimed timbers. I liked the idea of using a dark tone to contrast with the lighter color of the limestone floor. And for the spaces in between—the bookcases and the framed opening from the living room to the stair—I chose bleached wood, all of it punctuated by high-gloss black on the doors and doorframes. For the fireplace I found an old stone mantel from England that looked like one you might see in a Park Avenue lobby from the 1920s.

Because of the tight proportions of the main entrance, to gain access I knew that all of the furniture would have to be hoisted onto the terrace from the street below. This meant I really had to decide on everything by move-in day. Aesthetically, I was drawn to things that would blend seamlessly with the outside space and have a weathered look. The wood console, which I found on the Internet, might be the best expression of this. It was Belgian and had probably been sitting outdoors for a hundred years. It's still one of my favorite pieces.

Originally the apartment had three bedrooms, so we ended up taking one of the rooms and converting it into a dressing-area-cum-office and creating a two-room primary suite with a big bathroom, sealed off by pocket doors, at the top of the stair. To make space for the bathroom we combined two smaller ones, then placed a skylight directly over the tub and installed a big, glamorous shower clad in rustic shiny black tiles. We also raised the floor in this section of the apartment to mediate windows that just seemed to be placed too high in the wall.

RICHARD PHIBBS

ISAMU NOGUCHI
GREG GORMAN
VOLUME
VOGUE
PETER LINDBERGH
STORIES
MAASAI
VOGUE COVERS
Mrs. Newton
LUXURY TOYS
CANOVA

MAN RAY
A L'ÉTOILE SCELLÉE
DAY IS DONE
AFRICA

RIGHT: One concession to living with dogs is selecting a color palette that will help conceal animal hair—case in point the living room abaca, a perfect match to Lily's reddish coat. The coffee table is from Lucca Antiques in LA, the stool is African, and the draftsman's floor lamp is early twentieth century. Three exposures offer knockout views of sunrises and sunsets, plus full sun in the hours between—sunglasses frequently required.

MAN RAY
RICHARD PHIBBS

The bedroom curtains we'd had made for our previous apartment, so rather than just discard hundreds of yards of linen I recut them, added jute fringe, and hung them not only over the windows but the walls as well, tapestry-style. For the bed I designed a tall leather headboard that functioned as a kind of visual break from the fabric. It all came together pretty quickly, but the result was one of the coziest bedrooms ever. There was nothing better than lying on that bed as the setting sun lit up the sky and listening to the church bells peal the hour. Sometimes the sound of violins or cellos would even drift up from the music school. Talk about transporting!

In the back we created a guest bedroom suite, which also functioned as Brad's office and a TV room. A spacious daybed in brown leather and dotted with throw pillows in a variety of textures, floor-to-ceiling bookcases in weathered oak, and a plush Moroccan rug all contributed to making the small space maximally enveloping and cozy. I also covered the walls in brown velvet and used the same fabric for the curtains. It was a tiny room but super sexy thanks to all those textures and dark colors; a real escape. Life unfolded, and eventually we converted it into something quite the opposite—a pink-and-lavender bedroom for our daughter and later a nursery for our baby son.

For the kitchen, I was again inspired by what I was seeing in Northern Europe, such as the Belgian bluestone we used for the kitchen counters. I chose appliances with a shiny black finish, which I knew would make them recede visually. It's functional and minimalist yet still exudes the romance of a private garret. I loved that you could catch a glimpse of it from the living room without realizing that it was a kitchen, so it didn't disrupt the overall aesthetic. It was scarcely bigger than a wet bar, yet we managed to turn out some pretty ambitious meals in that little space, especially at Thanksgiving and Christmas. If Brad found he didn't have enough counter space, he'd just spread out onto the big table outside.

My dream for the terrace was to create one of those seductive spaces you might find at a small hotel in Rome or Paris. To that end I used a mixture of stalwart structural plants, like boxwood, with a variety of more tropical things that I'd introduce seasonally. And in the planter boxes we deployed a mix of birch trees for screening, as well as Moroccan roses whose brick-red color matched the building as well as the pair of terra-cotta–colored umbrellas that anchored either end of the space. We entertained out there a lot, and when the kids came along they'd play there with their friends.

I had fantasized about a place like this for so long that by the time we found it, I knew exactly what it should become. I remember feeling as though it had been waiting for me—an intuitive sensation I've experienced with most of the homes I've bought over the years. It was such a calming, peaceful environment I'd literally feel myself exhale as I walked through the door.

PREVIOUS PAGES, LEFT: The second-floor hallway proves the perfect place to hang art and photography gallery-style, not least because it's one spot in the light-abundant penthouse where the sun's rays won't reach.

PREVIOUS PAGES, RIGHT: The reclaimed fireplace mantel in the living room features four carved roses punctuating the crown and echoing the plantings on the terrace. Carolina's portrait is by photographer Richard Phibbs, a close family friend whose work appears throughout the apartment. The custom fireplace screen is tempered glass and sits on casters hidden beneath hammered pewter feet.

RIGHT: Before it was converted for use as Carolina's room, the second bedroom served as a guest room-cum-workspace with a custom daybed covered in saddle leather, walls and curtains of brown silk velvet, and a Moroccan carpet. The floor-to-ceiling bookcase is made from bleached white oak.

OVERLEAF, LEFT: Throughout the apartment a high-gloss black, oil-based paint is deployed on select doors as well as the powder room walls, adding some drama and serving as a counterpoint to all the rustic pieces and organic materials. The hardware is hammered silver.

OVERLEAF, RIGHT: The powder room off the entry hall provides a glamorous spot for a collection of black-and-white photography, including works by Patrick Demarchelier, Jim French, and Max Dupain, all safe here from direct sunlight.

PAGE 47: The kitchen counter is Belgian bluestone. Double doors lead directly onto the terrace's outdoor dining table, which seats fourteen.

PAGES 48–49: The dressing room features a mix of hang bars, shelving, and drawers, all hidden behind panels of bleached white oak millwork, while countertop surfaces are inset with black bridle leather.

PAGES 50–51: In the study, an armoire is retrofitted to open up as a work space for Brad—and sometimes Sid, a Labrador retriever who takes the business of a being a dog very seriously.

HOLLYWOOD
BABYLON
GERONTIUS
MAPPLETHORPE
BRIGHTNESS FALLS
I Celebrate Myself
CARY GRANT
OUTERBRIDGE REACH
ROBERT STONE
THE LIVES OF JOHN LENNON
HEMINGWAY
THE NOVEL
SON OF A GRIFTER
THE HIDDEN HITLER
GERMS

HOW TO RAISE A BOY
Hillbilly Elegy
J. D. VANCE
ADAM SCHIFF

ON WRITING WELL
ONE
LOVE

ROSLUND &
HELLSTRÖM
THREE SECONDS

That Could
BURNETT
Beaty | Roberts
THE QUESTIONEERS
ROALD DAHL
A TO Z MYSTERIES
THE CANARY CAPER
THE BALD BANDIT
THE DEADLY DUNGEON
nickelodeon
AVATAR
SMOKE AND SHADOW
ANN M. MARTIN
THE BABY-SITTERS

The Toad

The Dragonfly

The Sparrow

I WANT GREAT CLIMATE
DiCAMILLO VAN DUSEN Mercy Watson to the Rescue CANDLEWICK PRESS
Sullivan • Yoo Kitten and the Night Watchman SIMON & SCHUSTER
THE SEVEN SILLY EATERS Harcourt
THANK YOU, OMU!
/WABER HMCo
HENKES CHESTER'S WAY GREENWILLOW
Peter Brown The Curious Garden Little, Brown
RINGGOLD TAR BEACH CROWN

PAGES 52-53: In the master bedroom a leather headboard extends to the ceiling, while floor-to-ceiling curtains wrap three walls, creating a romantic cocoon for sleeping and relaxing. Both the headboard and the curtains were repurposed from our previous loft in Tribeca.

PAGES 54–55: The tiny bathroom off the back bedroom packs an outsize punch thanks to graphic tiles sourced in Morocco.

PREVIOUS PAGES: A grid of Hugo Guinness lithographs adorns one wall of Carolina's bedroom.

LEFT: For its second life as a little girl's bedroom, the former brown velvet from the back room walls is stripped and replaced with a mural inspired by a ceramic artwork purchased in Venice, California. The silver mercury reading lamp was found at the Paris flea market.

OVERLEAF: The existing arches in the terrace brickwork inspired us to install French doors—the better to capitalize on the view of St. Mark's, the second-oldest church in Manhattan. Tar paper, which had previously lined the terrace floor, was replaced with French limestone while the perimeter of the space was fitted out with teak planter boxes. Garden plantings include boxwood, birch trees, Moroccan roses (that often bloom well into November) and, along the pergola, wisteria that finally produced a desired canopy of green after several years of growth. Between the church view, the relatively low height of the surrounding buildings, and the treetop-level terrace, it's easy to feel as if you've been transported to a European garret.

CAPTAIN JACK'S WHARF
PROVINCETOWN

I first started visiting Provincetown in the mid-1990s, with Brad and our Labrador retriever, Stanley. There's a freewheeling, creative spirit to the town that instantly appealed to me. I also loved that it had this long history as a destination for artists and writers.

Captain Jack's Wharf reflects all of that in spades, which is probably why we immediately gravitated to it. The Wharf comprises a series of fishermen's cabins from the early nineteenth century that extend on pilings two hundred feet into Provincetown Bay, and which were later converted into summer cottages of various shapes and sizes. The first time we stayed there, we had a not-great unit close to the road. One day Stanley got away from me and ran to the far end of dock. I'd never ventured out that far before because it always seemed a little off-limits somehow, but when I caught sight of the cabin at the very end, I remember thinking how beautiful and special it was. It was a bit ramshackle but the setting was dreamy, with the wind gusting around and water views on three sides. The experience stayed with me over the years and the cabin became, to my mind, the ultimate Provincetown destination.

Fifteen or twenty years later, I was having dinner with a friend who had just returned from Provincetown. He started describing a property he had fallen in love with, and I quickly realized it was the very same cabin. I told him I knew it well and had also admired it. He said, "It's for sale. Let's buy it." And so we did.

When we got our hands on the place a year or so later it was a bit run-down, which only heightened our resolve and excitement. I'm always in favor of retaining natural patina where I can, but that doesn't extend to floors coated with so many layers of old oil-based paint that they're curling up in stiff shards, as was the case here. Even in its dilapidated state, though, the cabin seemed to me the ultimate salty dog hideaway. I liked the whole rustic vibe and the sense that this was a place with some history. In fact, rumor has it that Tennessee Williams spent a lot of time here in the '40s and even rehearsed his plays in the cottage. It also felt unmistakably nautical in a very natural way—enhanced by the view of Long Point Light Station, the historic lighthouse across the bay. My goal was to amplify the mood. I wanted to keep the weathered quality of the place and continue to chronicle and celebrate its long life, but to make it more comfortable and pulled together.

One of the first tasks was to sand the floors so we could see what colors had been used there over the years. I told the painter not to strip it down to the bare wood planks, but to even out the layers so we could keep them visible. Then we added some splattered paint on top and sealed it all so it would feel good under bare feet. At some point a mural of the wharf had been painted on the living room wall and, of course, we also wanted to protect that and make sure it remained a focal point.

Many of the design decisions were made based on the similar desire to retain elements

PAGES 68–69: Perched at the end of a 200-foot wharf, the cottage is virtually one with the elements, so a key consideration in the choice of furnishings was how they would age in the sun and salt air. Upholstery, too, was chosen with an eye for comfort, while still being rugged enough to hold up under wet dogs and bathing suits. Sliding doors allow the unit to pivot from maximum privacy to true indoor/outdoor living.

RIGHT: A variety of found pieces—a rattan sofa, a cupboard and end table painted in the same aqua hue, a mirror framed with bits of driftwood—underscore the cottage's sense of history. The tight color palette of blues and whites keeps things fresh yet still in tune with the nautical vibe of the wharf. Large leather armchairs and a wicker sofa strewn with throw pillows provide ample opportunity for reading, lounging, or just enjoying the view of the water and the Long Point Lighthouse beyond. The large Noguchi lantern that hangs over the center of the room is in perpetual motion as it catches the breeze off the water. A seagrass rug anchors the room and echoes the color of the surrounding weathered wood deck.

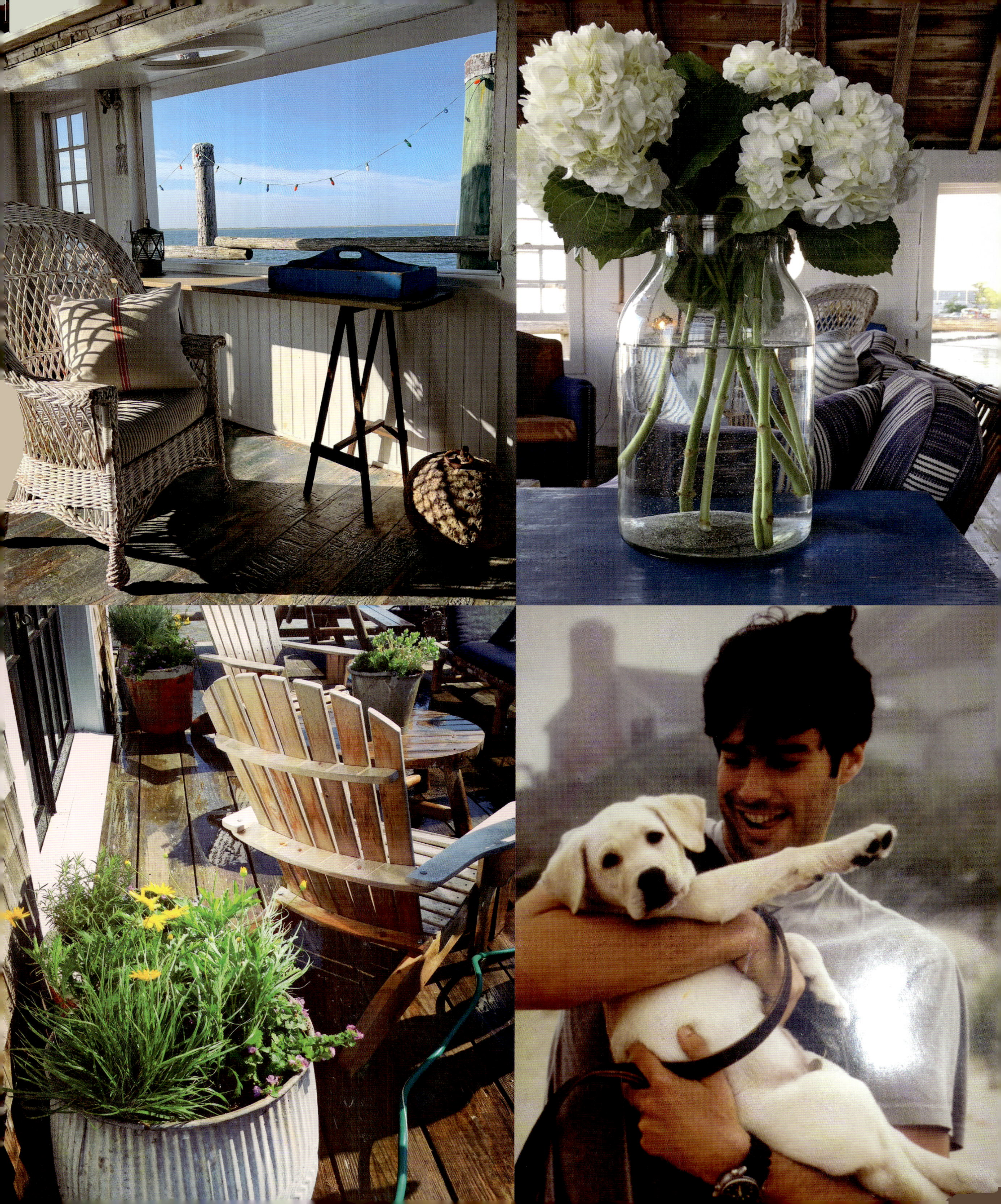

that we knew would continue to age beautifully. For instance, we added galvanized countertops in the kitchen–a material that's rustic but attractive and looked like it could have always been there. To replace a plastic shower stall in the bathroom, I bought one of those big porcelain pans from England and an old wall-mounted sink—I like it when you can't immediately tell whether something is new or antique. I wanted it all to be dramatic and cinematic; like you'd been transported out of modern life and onto the set of an old movie.

As for the decorative elements, my goal was to select pieces that would look as though they'd been collected over time—not like someone had spent the weekend blitz shopping the local flea markets. It needed found objects, but ones that felt considered and that told a story. Blue and white seemed the perfect principal colors to deploy, but I also wanted pops of other colors to keep it feeling natural. To that end, I injected red and blue via an old flag hung in the bedroom and in various throw pillows and the bathroom window shade, made from old hopsacks. And then there's the brown leather of the English club chairs in the living room, which look like they could have just been left behind by some previous resident—a writer or an artist, perhaps.

There are also plenty of weathered pieces in shades of sea green and brown, all of which feel nautical and like they've long been part of the cabin's colorful history. And from the living room ceiling I hung a big Noguchi lantern, which always makes me feel like the moon has drifted over from the night sky into our cottage. Since the kitchen is open to the living room it was important that whatever we placed there work within the context of the overall space; I've always loved blue splatterware from Bennington Potters in Vermont and it works perfectly here. Bright bunches of flowers keep it all fresh and happy—a big vase of sunflowers purchased at the local Stop & Shop always makes my day. It's all very cheerful and summery with an unabashedly American aesthetic.

Together the cabin and its surroundings coalesce into something uniquely romantic, like you've stepped back in time. The cottage came with plenty of charm; I just personalized it to fulfill my own fantasy of what I think a summer cabin perched on the water should feel like. Most of all it's a place where you feel very connected to the natural world. At the far end of the cottage there's a pair of sliding barn doors that can be pushed open so the end of the dock becomes an extension of the living room and you feel as if you're on the prow of a ship as it slices through the water. The wind comes in off the sea and blows the sheer curtains around like a sail and makes the Noguchi lantern swing on its chain. And at high tide there's the sound of the water lapping mere inches beneath the floorboards. It all feels intensely private, as though you're out on a boat—the wharf may be bustling, yet because of the cabin's location at the end of the dock you feel quite removed. It's the perfect spot to observe whatever is happening out on the water, or the sky at sunset, or the boats resting on the seabed when the tide goes out.

PAGE 76: Vintage Tolix café chairs in galvanized metal and zinc kitchen countertops were selected with an eye to developing a patina—sooner rather than later given the coastal setting's salt air. The dining table is vintage Lloyd Loom. Open shelving in the kitchen makes a small space feel almost expansive and presents an opportunity to display a collection of classic blue-and-white splatterware ceramics from Bennington Potters in Vermont. In lieu of drawers, under counter storage is provided via vintage wicker baskets.

OPPOSITE: The hatch window, which opens in toward the exposed A-frame ceiling on a rustic rope pulley, is said to have once served as a spot for fisherman to sell the day's catch. At night a simple shade made from an old hopsack is lowered over the hatch's porthole; come morning it's simply rolled up and tied in place. An antique wicker armchair from Maine with maximum patina and fresh blue-and-white upholstery keeps things easy and relaxed.

OVERLEAF: The sleeping loft is a cozy spot with a killer view of the sunrise, though a sleep mask is advised for those who don't want to rise at first light. A large iron cleat at the top of the stair is a thematic touch that also provides a little insurance when heading to bed after a late night of stargazing. Lighthouses are in abundance here, scaled-down table lamp versions included.

RIGHT: Bathroom fixtures were selected with the goal of making things feel in keeping with the cottage's past, so a vintage sink was installed in one corner and an English porcelain shower stall in the other. In lieu of closets, hooks and peg racks offer ample spots to stow shorts, T-shirts, and bathing suits—you don't need much more here. At night the bedroom shutters are closed to offer privacy while a ceiling fan keeps things cool and comfy.

OVERLEAF: A vintage American flag anchors the principal bedroom and introduces a bold shot of color—and a reminder that, in Provincetown, it's always the Fourth of July. Bedside tables assembled from driftwood and a table lamp wrapped in jute offer subtle connections to the watery landscape that surrounds. To the right of the bed, a secondary shower opens to the wharf and the ocean beyond—the ultimate room with a view.

DERING HARBOR COTTAGE
SHELTER ISLAND

After we'd had a house in East Hampton for close to twenty years, there came a point when we started to think about alternatives for where to spend our weekends and summer breaks—we knew we were going to be dads and were ready for something a little more mellow. Around that time, we were invited to lunch at a friend's place on Shelter Island. It felt so special that we reached out to a broker the next day. About six months later, he sent us a listing for a Victorian cottage in the village of Dering Harbor. We drove there on a beautiful summer Friday. It was late in the day and the house, which sits on a bluff overlooking the harbor and Gardiners Bay, was lit up like a lantern by the setting sun. It was glorious and took our breath away.

As a rule, I'm not a huge fan of Victorian architecture, but this one had less gingerbread than some. I loved its simplicity—it reminded me of an Edward Hopper painting. It needed a lot of work, though, so once we closed we had to push to get it done in time for the summer, which by then was just around the corner. We also had a newborn, so living there during construction wasn't really an option. It was all so rushed that my directions to the contractor never went much beyond "Paint it! Change it! Pull it out!" All the shingles had to be stripped. All the shutters removed. All the screen and storm windows fixed. The porch leveled. Trellises put in. New gutters. Wi-Fi and cable. New appliances across the board. We fixed the bathrooms, added lighting inside and out, removed a furnace from the basement that hadn't worked in a decade . . . We did a lot, and we did it fast.

Before taking on a major renovation I always recommend letting a house "talk" to you so you can understand what it really does or does not need. This is especially true for old houses, where new interventions that remove or damage original features may be difficult or impossible to restore. The challenge always is how to keep the patina and the authenticity while at the same time making it feel fresh and up-to-date. For example, sometimes it's best to just keep the old bathroom sinks but update the tile or paint. I'm typically drawn to homes where things have been allowed to age in place, and where there's a lived-in casualness to even the most formal spaces. I wanted Shelter Island to be the kind of place where the kids could run around barefoot and not worry about getting mud on the floors—which was the point of the seagrass rugs we use everywhere.

One pleasant discovery was that once we cut back some of the overgrown landscaping, we found that the front of the house was actually quite sunny and that the

ANNE PACKARD
Paul Cadmus The Male Nude
THE HAMPTONS
CHASING BEAUTY RICHARD PHIBBS
SEBASTIÃO SALGADO
GENESIS
TASCHEN
THE END MONTAUK, N.Y.
MICHAEL DWECK
TOM BARIL BOTANICA

three ground-floor rooms on that side were bathed in warm light. The last thing I wanted to do was to impede that in any way. But the house was also missing a front porch. It clearly had one once, probably a wraparound, but when we bought the place it was long gone and the front façade looked a bit like a face without a nose. The challenge was restoring that without blocking all the natural light. We compromised by adding a small, two-tiered porch to the front entrance. On the upper level we created a balcony that connected to the second floor's center bedroom via French doors—the perfect spot for watching the water or the weather rolling in. It made that bedroom really special—so of course Brad and I quickly claimed it for ourselves.

It actually took me a while to make this house feel like a home, and somewhat surprisingly it didn't have much to do with decorating the interiors per se. Two relatively simple things made the biggest impacts. First, the property had no hedges around the perimeter when we bought it, which meant no privacy, so when we finally added them the site no longer felt so exposed. That's when it all started to shift for me. Second was the simple addition of a porcelain farm sink and a marble counter to the kitchen island. With these two relatively small changes, everything began to feel a little more elevated. And then, of course, once we put in the pool it became our own happy little resort.

One thing I loved immediately was the screened-in side porch, which faces the harbor. Before we even closed, I found a great Victorian dining table with a zinc top and ornate wood legs in the perfect size. From the start I envisioned filling the porch with white wicker, which I knew I could find at the flea market in Brimfield, Massachusetts. It was amazing to see it all come together as a real outdoor room, especially when we added rugs and floor lamps. In the late afternoon and evening the breeze tends to pick up along the harbor; there's nothing better than sitting on one of the wicker sofas out there, listening to the wind chimes. At times it feels like being in one of those old Shingle Style cottages along the northern coast of Maine, something Brad picked up on the first time he laid eyes on the place, having spent some memorable summers there as a kid.

I always like a house whose rooms reflect the tones you can see on the exterior, which in this case meant relating furnishings to the green-and-white striped porch awnings visible from every window in the living and family rooms, as well as all the shades of green in the surrounding trees and the grass. Luckily, I find greens very soothing and relaxing. A green sofa in the summer feels fresh; toss a throw blanket on

HOTEL STORIES
ST. BARTHS
ST. TROPEZ
ROYAL HOLIDAYS
ASPEN
LAS VEGAS
A PRIVILEGED LIFE
A PRIVILEGED LIFE
HAMPTONS
PARIS HOTEL STORIES
SURF CONTEST
RON CHURCH

TRUMAN CAPOTE

HOTEL STORIES
ST BARTHS
ST TROPEZ
ROYAL HOLIDAYS
ASPEN
LAS VEGAS
A PRIVILEGED LIFE
A PRIVILEGED LIFE
HAMPTONS
PARIS HOTEL STORIES
CARY GRANT
ANNE PACKARD
Paul Cadmus The Male Nude
THE HAMPTONS

it in the fall and it turns cozy. In fact, the more we layered the house with that palette the better it started to feel.

One of the decisions I made early on was to use the designated dining room in a different way. As originally laid out it was right off the screened-in porch, in the spot where an outdoor dining table would naturally sit, which meant there would have been two long tables and their corresponding lineup of chairs in adjacent spaces—useless except for meals. Shifting the inside dining area to a more intimate room farther away allowed the original dining room to function as a kind of family room. Now it gets constant use by the kids and we can have family breakfasts there. During the warm months we mostly eat dinner on the porch anyway, so we made sure the "new" dining room would feel cozy in colder months. It ended up being a good move and helped us to truly optimize the busiest spaces in the house.

The living room just evolved naturally, with a mix of pieces from East Hampton, landscape paintings (which I love), and odds and ends we've gathered over time. Initially the room's proportions felt slightly awkward—because it's a bit narrow the seating areas had to be placed far from each other, but I wanted to make the space feel more conducive to conversation. I ended up finding a large, rectangular coffee table to fill the empty floor space, loaded it up with books and objects, and it somehow balances the room and makes everything feel closer and more unified.

Upstairs, I felt I had more latitude to play with different ideas, in part because you don't see the kids' rooms in the back from the principal rooms up front. That gave me license to try something else there in terms of color and pattern: wallpaper. I think the house would have turned stodgy quickly if we hung too much of it, but using it in isolated areas felt really good—in tune with the era but still at ease.

Given the house's location I'd known we'd have the pleasure of watching the ferry travel between Greenport and Shelter Island year-round, but I wasn't aware of what a sailor's haven Dering Harbor is, or the fact that we'd have a front-row seat to all the races and other sailboat activity happening around us. We're also treated to the sight of these and other boats, many of them incredibly majestic, anchored right outside our door. This happens throughout the summer, with a number of them arriving during the night so they become a surprise addition to the next day's backdrop. It's an ever-changing vista—sometimes a huge sloop, others a major yacht—and at night they tend to be all lit up, with the twinkling lights reflected on the water. It's pure magic.

NEW YORK 1880
IN MY SKIN
BOYS
ROTELLA
Seydou Keïta
HIDE SEEK

WINNER/JURY GRAND PRIZE VENICE INTERNATIONAL FILM FESTIVAL
WINNER/Best Actor (Coppa Volpi) JAVIER BARDEM VENICE INTERNATIONAL FILM FESTIVAL
BEFORE
A FILM BY JULIAN SCHNABEL

PAGES 98–99: A vintage wicker table found in Sag Harbor offers the ideal spot for conveniently storing footwear and other items at the base of the stair. A pendant light by Robert Ogden is fashioned from various vintage elements, and striped indoor/outdoor runners by Dash & Albert help to create a sense of calm and cohesion in the upper hallway.

PAGES 100–101: The antique coffee table—most likely an old worktable whose legs were shortened—helps to anchor the living room and balance its somewhat narrow proportions. The nineteenth-century Danish side chair was found in Hudson, New York. A portrait of Carolina by family friend Anastasia Egeli receives pride of place between French doors that open on to the screen porch facing Gardiners Bay. The sofa and club chairs are by George Sherlock, and the striped fabric in shades of green, which appears throughout the house, is by Bennison.

PREVIOUS SPREAD: In the entry, a painted eighteenth-century French secretary found at the Paris flea market commands center stage and takes the place of a coal-burning fireplace that originally occupied the spot. The Ralph Lauren wing chairs are a popular spot for reading.

OPPOSITE: The work of artist Hugo Guinness is a favorite and can be found throughout the house. A framed poster of Julian Schnabel's *Before Night Falls* is a treasured item, both because of the film's subject matter and the artist's fading inscription scrawled across the top. Entry walls are covered in a Ralph Lauren grasscloth.

OVERLEAF: We designated a smaller room for use as our dining room, finding the original too large for daily use; now this room functions as both a library and a workspace as well as a spot for large dinners when the weather turns cool. The dining table and bookcase are from Ralph Lauren, and the dining chairs are custom Alfredo Paredes Studio.

PAGES 116–117: We turned the original dining room into a family room. Wicker seating by Bielecky Brothers, two kid-size chairs, and a long coffee table make it a favorite spot for family breakfast. The carved birds are from the Black Forest region of Germany, and the leather floor lamps are by Jacques Adnet. The pottery was sourced over many years at various flea markets and chosen for the varied shades of green, with most of it dating from the 1930s and '40s.

PAGE 119: The black-and-white portraits of Alfredo and our dogs, Sid and Lily, are by close family friend Richard Phibbs.

HAWAII SURF
SHAPED BY
Minami
Paddy Clarke
LOVE, etc.
Garcia
STRANGE PIECE of PARADISE
Living to Tell
THE INFORMANT
Intimate Connections
Turtle Moon

Minami

LONG ISLAND, NEW YORK
CLOSE TO NATURE
The Children's Garden
SURVIVAL WISDOM
& KNOW-HOW

PRODUCTOS CASAMIGOS DE AGAVE
CLASE
Blanco
CATEGORIA
Tequila 100%
Agave Azul
HECHO
Jalisco, Mexico
NUMERO 23118
CASAMIGOS
Tequila
EXCLUSIVO

PREVIOUS PAGES: The installation of new Victorian-style hardware, marble counter tops, and a porcelain farm sink keeps the kitchen feeling fresh yet still in harmony with the historic era of the house. The green color scheme also carries over into the kitchen, where a sage-colored Farrow and Ball paint covers a portion of each wall, creating the illusion of wainscoting. The pendant light is nineteenth-century English.

OPPOSITE: A vintage American cupboard serves as a pantry and helps to resolve a lack of storage in the existing kitchen layout. Original hardware, drawers, and cabinetry in the butler's pantry are given new life thanks to the addition of marble countertops, bronze sink fixtures from Rohl, and antique sconces found in LA. The table lamp is by Robert Ogden.

OVERLEAF: The absence of a powder room on the ground floor was ultimately resolved by the conversion of a small hallway and coat closet that conveniently already contained a window. A high-gloss, oil-based Farrow and Ball paint in hunter green applied to the shiplap walls ensures the space feels intimate yet never claustrophobic. The English pedestal sink is from Drummonds and the lighting is from Urban Archeology.

PAGES 126–127: Grasscloth and a blue-striped fabric, both from Ralph Lauren, bring a dash of seaside serenity to one of the two guest bedrooms. Vintage throw pillows and a Pendleton blanket complete the look. The sconces are from Schoolhouse Electric.

MAP SHOWING
THE WATERWORKS SYSTEMS OF
LONG ISLAND, NEW YORK

OPPOSITE: With views of the harbor from every window, it's tempting to simply pull up a chair and watch the world drift past. The folk art table with original paint is nineteenth-century American, found at the flea market in Brimfield; it ultimately drove the blue color scheme here.

OVERLEAF: Once the front porch with its second-floor balcony was added, there was no question we'd claim the center bedroom as our own. With the doors ajar and a breeze coming in off the water, it's not unlike being aboard a ship. The vintage English chair is by Howard & Sons. The bed is custom Alfredo Paredes Studio, topped with a blanket from Pendleton. This bedroom, which also functions as a pass-through to the kids' rooms in the rear, was originally set up as a quiet workspace, with an old Victorian table serving as a desk and striped Roman shades in a Ralph Lauren fabric.

PAGES 134–135: Botanically inspired photography and artwork are evident throughout the house, including in one of the two guest rooms, where a Hugo Guinness drawing of wildflowers is perched beside a tulip photograph by an unknown artist. The bureau is nineteenth-century French and still retains its original paint.

PREVIOUS PAGES: A pair of vintage French armchairs covered in fabric salvaged from hopsacks sit at the foot of one of the guestroom beds—the ideal spot for conversation or contemplation.

OPPOSITE: Carolina does some journaling on the playroom daybed. The throw pillow is from John Derian, and the curtain fabric is by Ralph Lauren.

OVERLEAF: In Sebastian's room, a playful approach to all things nautical keeps the space fun, yet snug and serene. A navy paper depicting the celestial skies adorns the walls, while a variety of nautically themed art and objects provides an abundance of personality. The bedroom rug is by Dash & Albert. The blue-and-white paper lantern in the hall is Noguchi. Stuffies and a Pendleton blanket draped across the foot of the bed provide shots of color—made all the more vivid against the deep blue backdrop.

PAGES 142–143: For Carolina's room, a lighter shade of blue with pale pink accents take things in a more feminine direction. The wallpaper is by Ralph Lauren, and the blue-and-white throw pillows are vintage. The figurative artwork is by Hugo Guinness; the abstract is an early work by Carolina herself.

CMP

Chart 14
THE CLOVE HITCH
MADE IN THE CENTER OF A ROPE
Chart 8
SQUARE KNOT
USED TO JOIN TWO ROPES OF EQUAL SIZES.
STANDING PART
RUNNING END
RUNNING END
STANDING PART

MATILDA
Provost and Stockwell
GOOD NIGHT STORIES REBEL GIRLS
A Velocity of Being

OVERLEAF: Rodeo lights strung outside the kitchen and porch give the house a perpetually fun and festive vibe. The striped awnings have been a feature of the house for decades and make a vivid statement from the water. Evening light imbues the house with a golden glow.

Times Like These
A to Z Wineworks Oregon Chardonnay
2018 $12.97
Bodegas Ponce Manchuela Clos Lojen
Bobal 2018 $10.87

OPPOSITE: The home's biggest selling point, and the space that's undoubtedly used the most, is the screened-in porch. Alfredo bought the large Victorian zinc-topped dining table before we'd even closed on the house, immediately registering the size as perfect for the space. In the evening it provides the ideal spot to gather over a meal and enjoy the sunset, while during the day it provides a front-row seat to frequent sailboat races. Vintage Tolix chairs in zinc were purchased at the Paris flea market, and the dishes are by Burleigh and Ralph Lauren.

OVERLEAF: No one appreciated the beauty of Shelter Island or the dramatic location of the house more than our dogs, Sid and Lily—their forever happiest place. The lawn abutting the harbor is a frequent spot for bonfires and s'mores. The stairs lead down the hill to a deep-water dock.

COCUYO
LOCUST VALLEY

Like so many other families, we had an impulse to reevaluate our living situation in New York City when the pandemic hit. We were lucky to have our Shelter Island place as an escape from the virus, and during the extended time we spent there we saw how much happier and more comfortable we all were than we'd been during the months prior, in our East Village apartment. The impact of simply having the space to spread out a bit both indoors and out was eye-opening. We clearly needed more room. Though we love the city, I knew how challenging it was going to be to find a comparable apartment with additional square footage. So, for a couple of years my bedtime routine involved flipping open my laptop and obsessively scouring online real estate listings for whatever town within commuting distance of the city I'd zeroed in on for the night.

What immediately became clear was that whether I was looking at Chestnut Hill in Philadelphia, Bronxville, the Hudson Valley, or Connecticut, I inevitably found myself drawn to English-style houses built in the 1920s. They tend to feel very elegant yet somehow ineffably masculine as well. And despite often being large, their interiors are usually well proportioned with an easy flow from room to room, which translates to warm and inviting. This house had all of that, though what caught my eye initially was the fact that it had been designed by Harrie T. Lindeberg, an architect I've long admired. We arranged a viewing for the next day; knowing my weakness for plaster walls, arched doorways, and casement windows, as soon as we walked in Brad turned to me and said, "I guess we're moving."

The place also looks like something you'd see in an old Hollywood movie, which is always inspiring to me. And miraculously, all the original details were still intact. From the outset I loved the façade's roofline, the arched entry in the brick portico, the circular motor court, and the wide staircase running graciously from the entry hall to the second floor. I remember standing at the base of the stairs marveling at how such a big, formal house could also immediately feel so embracing.

During my decades working at Ralph Lauren we actually looked to Lindeberg's aesthetic often for inspiration. In fact, I wouldn't be at all surprised to learn that I had studied images of this very house over the years while working on various projects and installations. One thing I do know is that it reminded me in certain ways of our East Village apartment, though on a much bigger scale, so it felt very familiar. I guess that explains Brad's reaction on that first visit.

In reimagining the place, I definitely wanted to keep the sense that it was from another era, to respect the parts that alluded to history and made it feel established and solid but to avoid making it feel like a period piece. Take that front entry hall—instead of setting it up to be a static space you simply walk through on your way to somewhere else, we made sure it

PAGE 154: Architect Harrie T. Lindeberg, who designed this house in 1929, wasn't afraid of a little whimsy. Case in point: this antique lockset on the front door. To insert your key, you must flip up the knight's shield, attached via a tiny hinge. It's a tricky maneuver when you're carrying groceries, but charming all the same.

PREVIOUS PAGES: The home's façade has remained unchanged since it was built. That includes the lantern above the front archway, which hangs from the neck of a wrought-iron dragon. The roof tiles are terra-cotta, fabricated by Ludowici in Ohio—we've been told that the company still retains Lindeberg's original plans in their archives.

OPPOSITE: French doors connect the formal living room to the outdoor terrace. Individual panels in each of the two flanking windows are operable, presumably for airflow.

OVERLEAF, LEFT: A portrait of Alfredo's mother from the 1960s takes pride of place on an old English easel in the living room. The curtains are mohair velvet in a forest green.

OVERLEAF, RIGHT: An abstract ceramic sculpture sits on a mid-century French limed oak pedestal found in Paris. The chair is faux bois, from the 1930s.

PAGE 162: A view from the living room into a space Lindeberg dubbed "the loggia," an unheated, screened-in room that's perfect on a summer night. The pedestal to the right of the double doors is limed oak, and the vase that sits atop is mid-century American Art Pottery.

AMER
A.M.G. 1000 MODEL DIRECTORY
THE DETAILED INTERIOR
Mrs. Newton
FLOWER FLASH
FALLINGWATER
Do not disturb
BECOMING
VALENTINO
MIRABILIA
DIANA VREELAND
HOUSEHOLD IDOLS
OLYMPIA LENI RIEFENSTAHL
RICHARD
RICHARD PHIBBS
Alfred Stieglitz
Jack Pierson
PLAYERS
AMERICAN HOME
TIMELESS

LUCIAN FREUD
Rock and Royalty
TRACEY EMIN WORKS 2007-2017
kara walker
PETER MARINO
ART ARCHITECTURE

kara walker
TRACEY EMIN WORKS 2007–2017
MATTHEW ROLSTON
NEW YORK INTERIORS

THE RADICAL EYE
JULIA MARGARET CAMERON
Marella Agnelli The Last Swan
PHIBBS

PREVIOUS PAGES: In the living room, a black oak center table by Alfredo Paredes Studio is piled with books and objects, and the Santana sofa and club chairs by Alfredo Paredes Studio are covered in oatmeal linen—luxe, yet relaxed. The fabric of the striped pillow is by Zak + Fox. An antique oriental rug in shades of brown and moss is positioned over a sisal floor covering, anchoring the room and delivering some of the layered coziness associated with country house living. The black-and-white charcoal nude in the rear is by an unknown artist and was found at the Paris flea market.

OPPOSITE: Built-in bookcases in the living room were switched from their original dark brown to white in an effort to lighten the room; filled with art books and objets d'art, including an array of black-and-white photography, they become informal contemporary vignettes showcasing some favorite objects. Carolina's portrait is by close family friend Richard Phibbs.

OVERLEAF, LEFT: The living room's coffee table is piled with books and objects, including a modernist bronze sculpture of a man in prayer. The large ceramic vase is black basalt.

OVERLEAF, RIGHT: The console is nineteenth-century Portuguese and retains its original marble top. It's flanked by African stools in a similar tone—a harmonious mix despite dramatically different provenances. The charcoal drawing is by contemporary Spanish artist Aythamy Armas, in a vintage parcel gilt Spanish frame.

PAGE 172: The living room sofa is flanked by black iron floor lamps whose material recalls the dark lead used in the surrounding window frames.

Antique Tools and Instruments
L'invention du chic
BAND OF BIKERS
TOM BIANCHI
ON THE COUCH
Howard Roffman Pictures of Kris
GYPSET STYLE
ASSOULINE
MATTHEW BARNEY
Ezra Stoller Photographer
Yale
JEAN DUNAND
THE SEASIDE HOUSE LIVING ON THE WATER
New Asian Style
NEW ASIAN INTERIORS
eve arnold film journal
AN ATHLETE IN TIGHTS
LOST ANGELES
The Architecture of Japan
GREAT AMERICAN THING
MODERN ART AND NATIONAL IDENTITY, 1915-1935
RENE HERBST
DEBERG
GEORGE PLATT LYNES
exchange and transformation, 1910–1930
RALPH LAUREN
ANDY WARHOL'S EXPOSURES
PHOTOGRAPHERS' PARIS
Paul Klee Irony at work
PRESTEL
Walker Evans
The Hungry Eye
PIERRE VERGER

RICHARD PHIBB
AFRICA
HERB RITTS
CASE STUDY

CUBA
Outerbridge
Atget
PORTRAITS

Outerbridge

was a place where we might actually want to spend time and that would hold up to heavy use. For instance, our kids do a weekly karate class there with a few of their friends. Similarly, the living room is this very generous, elegantly proportioned room that you step down into to indicate a transition to a reception space. We use it in that way at times, of course, and love the heightened formality of the room, but by furnishing it with a wide and pillowy sofa and club chairs I ensured it would also be a comfy place to hang out when we weren't entertaining—in fact, that sofa has become my favorite quiet spot to take a nap. We wanted to be certain that in reimagining the house it would fit the realities of our lifestyle and not be restricted by how people lived in 1930.

The biggest change we made was moving the kitchen. The original kitchen was pretty uninteresting and obviously designed at a time when you would have had staff making your meals, so the owners probably never set foot in there. It clearly wasn't Lindeberg's highest design priority; now it functions beautifully as a pantry and secondary kitchen instead.

This tied in well to solving the riddle of how to use what we call "the great room." The space was conceived as an artist's studio for the original owner. A soaring, barrel-vaulted ceiling easily makes this room the most dramatic in the house, and therefore one that should be used daily. But we already had a beautiful living room and it felt too vast to work either as a study or TV room. The solution was to move the principal kitchen there. The idea of a kitchen-cum-family room where you can cook, eat, and gather to talk or read or watch TV is a very American, twenty-first century concept that makes a lot of practical sense. It also shifts the activity center of the house to what is arguably its most appealing space. Come by most any evening and that's where you're likely to find us.

In terms of furniture, I knew we'd need larger-scaled pieces than the ones we'd been living with in the city. And because there's more space for things to stand on their own, I was able to go for stronger, darker materials, like mahogany. We also used a lot of pieces from my own furniture collection; many of those designs were created while we were in the process of buying the property, so the house itself served as a source of inspiration. The result, naturally, is that they feel right at home. That said, there's a modernity and a freshness to the place that I wanted to maintain by keeping things on the more minimal side.

Adapting the formal dining room to fit how we actually live also took thought. It's a huge space, so any dining table large enough to fill it would have needed many leaves—always a hassle to install and remove. I ended up designing a sixteen-foot-long dining table in quarter-sawn oak, which is big enough to fill the room proportionally, yet managed not to feel overly formal. We've had some great, fun dinners there—including Christmas, when we hosted eighteen

Paul Jasmin
DAY IS DONE
Alpine Interiors

TASCHEN
THE WORLD OF GLORIA VANDERBILT
WENDY GOODMAN
ROMAN AND WILLIAMS BUILDINGS AND INTERIORS
THINGS WE MADE
FOCUS
Beaumont Newhall
THE WORLD OF DOWNTON ABBEY
JESSICA FELLOWES
PAVEL TCHELITCHEV
ANTHONY GOICOLEA
David Doubilet
Water Light Time

PREVIOUS PAGES: The Steinway baby grand is from the 1930s; it was purchased with the house but underwent a full-scale restoration. The portrait of the man in the upper left is by Sheila Metzner. The sconce, one of a set of four, is original to the house. The black-and-white photo perched in the bookcase is of musician Jakob Dylan, by Mark Seliger.

OPPOSITE: Books can be a key component of every room, but bookcases look great when filled with many things—books, for sure, but art and objects as well. According to Alfredo, the key is to keep it organic and to add to it over time.

OVERLEAF: A mix of art and photography fills the house. The male nude is by Horst. The propeller shot is by an unknown artist.

PAGES 180–181: A view into the living room reveals an abstract lithograph above the fireplace. We changed a number of the fireplace mantels throughout the house because we felt other materials or designs would work better, but this one is original and inspired the decision to introduce various types of stone elsewhere in the house.

PAGE 182: The second-floor landing originally had an elevator (we hypothesize more for easy movement of steamer trunks than people), which emerged from the floor. Now, an English library table with a granite top occupies the spot, great for plants given the large window in the stairwell, which features a handful of stained-glass panels. The space is punctuated by a large iron lantern from Spain that made the move from our apartment in the East Village.

SEXMACHINE by Lalli
EDITION E/ROS
Lalli X SEXBOMB!
WHEN WE WERE THREE
AMG 1000 MODEL DIRECTORY
AMG 1000 MODEL DIRECTORY 2
100 UNFORGETTABLE DRESSES HAL RUBENSTEIN
THE DETAILED INTERIOR DECORATING UP CLOSE WITH CULLMAN & KRAVIS
Andy Warhol Nudes
LENGTHENING SHADOWS BEFORE NIGHTFALL
AT HOME WITH MAY AND AXEL VERVOORDT
Flammarion
FRANCOIS HALARD
VISITE PRIVEE
PORTRAITS
Warhol by Galella That's Great!
COUNTRY STYLE
California Mediterranean
June Newton a.k.a. Alice Springs
Mrs. Newton
VOYEUR
FLOWER FLASH
KAUFMANN FALLINGWATER ABBEVILLE
Gianni Versace Do not disturb
ANNIE LEIBOVITZ AT WORK
RANDOM HOUSE
JACK PIERSON SELF PORTRAIT
WWD
BOND

PAGES 184–185: The view from the entry hall into the dining room. This doorway existed in the original design but featured recessed pocket doors, which we removed to keep things open. The nineteenth-century French wing chair is one of a pair and is flanked by a black iron floor lamp chosen for its slightly ecclesiastical attitude.

PREVIOUS PAGES: A dining room of such large proportions required some bold moves, such as the decision to cover the walls in a scenic paper by Fine & Dandy depicting trees and rolling hills—a subconscious echo of the view just outside. The curtains are teal mohair velvet and the dining table, in quarter-sawn oak, is custom Alfredo Paredes Studio. Sconces, one of a set of four, are black iron.

OPPOSITE: A broad chaise, which made the journey from the East Village terrace, is now flanked by two faux bois side tables and sits outside the dining room window. The glass orbs are lanterns filled with citronella oil—a romantic touch that also helps to keep the mosquitoes away.

OVERLEAF: In the loggia, four frescoes by Frederic Edwin Church of birdcages—populated by a variety of white birds—flank the French doors to the exterior as well as the facing window. In addition to being an heir to the Arm & Hammer fortune, Church, who commissioned the house and was its original occupant, was a well-regarded painter of his time (he signed his work F. Edwin Church to avoid confusion with another painter of the same name). He also painted the trompe l'oeil brickwork surrounding the mirrors and French doors. The sofa and chairs are contemporary wicker, while the Baja coffee table is by Alfredo Paredes Studio.

PAGES 192–193: The loggia leads to a covered outdoor dining area. The table lamp is vintage folk art.

PAGES 194–195: The room with the vaulted wood ceiling was, we believe, originally designed as a space for Church to paint large canvases. We converted it into a multipurpose great room, with separate zones for cooking, dining, and gathering to talk or watch TV. The pendant lamps are by Jamb, from London, and the chairs are by Alfredo Paredes Studio.

PAGES 196–197: The banquette in the dining area is covered in a striped performance fabric. The woven chairs are by Alfredo Paredes Studio. The counters are Calacatta viola marble from Southern Italy. The range is by Lacanche, and the hood is custom.

THE HIGH LINE
DISFARMER
PARIS
Dressing in the Dark
FICTIONS

(without running short on counter space, as we did in the East Village). Large rooms also mean plenty of wall space; to make this one feel inviting and cohesive, I ended up installing a beautiful scenic wallpaper, something that's a bit of a stylistic departure for me. The choice of a pastoral image for the space has the effect of bringing the surrounding woods into the room. It feels very considered when I explain it, but it was actually intuitive—I really just liked the image.

It's funny, but I don't think someone coming into the house today would register that we did all that much to the place—and that was the goal. In truth, most of the work we did involved subtle updates, like installing new lighting and speakers hidden in the ceiling, central AC, repairing the chimneys, adding closet space, and lots of repainting. Those speakers were especially key for me, as music—Billie Holliday, Van Morrison, Miles Davis—is such an important part of how I set the mood.

Ironically, there were a lot of details original to the house that I ended up redoing in a similar style, to my mind making them more in tune with the period and appropriate to the quality of the architecture. Some of the doors were hollow, for example, so they didn't match the overall standards of the original design. Brad joked that several of the bathrooms looked like ones you might have seen in a Depression-era municipal building, so we redid those in a style and with materials that felt in step with Lindeberg's vision. I also wanted things more in keeping with the country-house feeling I was picking up and that I felt could be enhanced.

I certainly didn't want any of the changes I made to compete with the inherent beauty of the architecture. That's not to say I didn't alter a few details: I added arched doorframes to create a sense of continuity between rooms, raised a few others that seemed too low, and added doors at either end of the second-floor hall to make it feel cozier and more private—all things aimed at making it feel like an inviting and well-appointed country residence. And we also ended up giving the house a new name, Cocuyo, which means "firefly" in Spanish—a nod to both my Cuban heritage and the way the house's leaded-glass windowpanes twinkle at night.

After almost two years, I realize the move here has been everything I imagined and exactly what we needed as a family. When I pull into Locust Valley on the train, get into my car, drive through the little town, and pull up to our driveway, what I feel is contentment. That reaction tells me I made the right choice. The place feels spacious yet filled with life year-round. Plus I'm happy to be closer to nature—something I had missed during our many years of urban living. I like that I can grow things here and watch things change.

JIM BEAM
KENTUCKY STRAIGHT
BOURBON
WHISKEY
OBAN
14
12
ST-RÉMY
VSOP
FRENCH BRANDY FRANÇAIS
COURVOISIER
V·S
SASSICAIA
2020
BOLGHERI SASSICAIA
HOT

Tito's
Handmade
VODKA
AUSTIN TEXAS
GIN
OFFLEY
RUBY PORTO
NOILLY PRAT
1813
VERMOUTH
ORIGINAL FRENCH DRY
MARTINI & ROSSI
1863
MARTINI
ROSSO
CÓDIGO
1530
PAMPERO

complete
ravel
THE WORLD'S GREATEST VIOLIN CONCERTOS

male nudes

SURFING SAN ONOFRE TO POINT DUME
1936-1942
PHOTOGRAPHS BY DON JAMES
NEW YORK
AL DIGEST
October 21, 2014
Dear Alfredo & Brad,
It was so special sharing my birthday with you in Paris, and the flowers you sent were really extraordinary. Know how much I value our friendship and the times like this we get to spend together.
Love,
Ralph

RICHARD
RALPH LAUR
ML 4520

PAGES 198–199: Open oak shelving provides an opportunity to display a collection of ceramics and wicker baskets. The sink fixtures are by Waterworks.

PAGES 200–203: A wet bar adjacent to the living room was simplified and streamlined with Titanium stone countertops. The same material was also deployed for a matching backsplash and open shelving, while undercounter storage is hidden behind cabinets of waxed white oak. The sink hardware is by Waterworks. The black-and-white photograph is by Bruce Weber.

PAGES 204–205: A studio in the home's lower level provides a workspace for Alfredo, but the sectional, by Alfredo Paredes Studio, is also a great spot for watching movies. The black-and-white painting above the door is by artist Joseph La Piana, a close family friend. The paper floor lamp is Noguchi.

PREVIOUS PAGES: Alfredo's desk is 1940s French and is flanked by an early-twentieth-century floor lamp that made the move from the East Village. The photography wall features work by Herb Ritts and McDermott & McGough, as well as a charcoal portrait of Alfredo's father, from the 1960s.

OPPOSITE: A coffee table by Alfredo Paredes Studio holds a casually curated collection of books and objects. Ceramics and carved wood pieces are always a favorite of Alfredo's.

HOTEL LACHAPELLE
NIGHTVISIONS
Wouter Deruytter Cowboy Code
HIP HOTELS BEACH
THE TIMES SQUARE GYM

TAKE IVY

PAGES 210–211: The fireplace in the studio, with its original integrated stone surround, makes for a cozy corner to work or relax. The club chairs are 1930s French, still covered in their original red leather. The bookcases are by Alfredo Paredes Studio and work as a catchall for books and other objects. Art and photography in a variety of scales and featuring a range of subjects adorns the studio, hung as well as stacked. The painting is by Alexandre Kasproviez.

OPPOSITE: A portrait of Alfredo from the early 1990s, by photographer David Seidner.

OVERLEAF: Details from around the home illustrate Alfredo's love of rusticity.

PAGES 218–219: The entry called for something big: a multi-drawer shop counter from nineteenth-century Italy fit the bill exactly. The sconces are by Jamb, and the vase is by Natan Moss.

PAGE 221: A nineteenth-century wing chair flanks an English Arts and Crafts side table at the base of the stair and has become a favorite spot for making calls and answering emails.

ANNIE LEIBOVITZ
TASCHEN
DAVID YARROW STORYTELLING

naked men too
UNIVERSE

OPPOSITE: A Portuguese stained oak table found in the South sits at the base of the stairs leading to the studio. The Man Ray exhibition announcement is French, and was purchased at the Paris flea market.

OVERLEAF: To create a greater sense of privacy in the second-floor hallway, oak paneled double doors were added, designed to match Lindeberg's original specifications. A cinnamon-colored sisal runner extends the length of the hallway and down the main stairs. The pendant light is by Jamb. The artwork at left is one half of a pair of nineteenth-century Japanese screens.

PAGES 226–229: In the primary bedroom, the goal was to create a cocooning space that would equal our East Village bedroom in warmth and coziness. To that end an oatmeal-colored plush wool rug anchors the room, while a mahogany-colored mohair velvet is used for the bed's headboard. Continuing a theme, the curtains have been recycled for a third time, having made the move from our bedroom in the city after originally being hung in our Tribeca loft. The chairs are George Sherlock and are covered in a ginger-colored rough-out suede. The oak console in the bay window is nineteenth-century English, while the bedside lamp is 1930s ceramic. The limestone fireplace mantel is 1930s French; it replaces a wood original. Black-and-white photography on the windowsill and on the wall is by Richard Phibbs.

MAN RAY
Vernissage le Mardi 24
à 21 heures
A L'ÉTOILE
11, RUE DU PRÉ-AUX

'51
J. VERVISCH.

OPPOSITE: A two-foot-high bronze statue of a boxer dates to the 1930s and made the move from our New York City dressing room. Today it sits happily in the window of the principal bath.

PAGES 234–237: In our bathroom, we created a shower "room" with a view over the garden and clad the surround in a dramatic Copacabana marble, with fixtures by Waterworks. The same marble is used to wrap the walls, as well. The black-and-white tile floor was inspired by the basketweave tile popular in bathrooms of the 1920s. To offset the black of the stone and introduce warmth, we installed a custom oak shelving unit inspired by barley twist antiques, which holds the double sinks and offers storage on the levels beneath. It's fitted with fixtures by Waterworks.

PAGES 238–239: In Brad's office off the great room, a floor-to-ceiling bookcase painted in a high-gloss Farrow and Ball brown holds an ever-expanding collection of books. A loose-weave grasscloth wallcovering provides texture. The desk is a vintage writing table.

PAGES 240–241: In the largest guest bedroom, an Alfredo Paredes Studio bed is covered in a mahogany mohair velvet while the double-height casement window is hung with curtains in a print fabric by Bennison. The scrubbed pine bureau is Belgian, and the sconce is English.

OPPOSITE: The principal bedroom suite has two walk-in closets. Surfaces are painted a high-gloss brown from Farrow and Ball—masculine yet reflective enough to bounce light around the room.

OVERLEAF: In Sebastian's bedroom, a blue-and-white striped paper from Farrow and Ball provides the perfect backdrop for a collection of favorite toys and objects, including an Italian movie poster purchased in Rome. His bunk beds were custom painted in a matte blue. The desk is a mid-century steel office desk, and the rug is indoor/outdoor from Dash & Albert. The bathroom is painted in a Farrow and Ball aquamarine, while the sink and fixtures are from Waterworks.

PAGE 251: Carolina's room reflects her favorite color, lilac, in a custom Alfredo Paredes Studio trundle bed covered in a mohair velvet, as well as the batik curtains and a block print wallpaper from Quadrille. The rug is performance.

PAGES 252–253: The laundry room was designed to include cubbies for kids' coats and sports equipment. The tongue-and-groove walls are painted in a high-gloss, steel-blue paint by Farrow and Ball, which keeps things fresh and offsets the black-and-white linoleum floor tiles. A nineteenth-century natural oak counter from France is repurposed as a folding table. (Its legs offered inspiration for the sink console in the master bathroom.)

CINETECA BOLOGNA
la SACHER FILM presenta
Il Cinema Ritrovato al cinema
Classici restaurati in prima visione
CARO DIARIO
un film di
NANNI MORETTI
con
NANNI MORETTI
RENATO CARPENTIERI
ANTONIO NEIWILLER
una coproduzione
SACHER FILM, ROMA • BANFILM-ARTE, PARIGI
CON LA COLLABORAZIONE DI
RAIUNO E CANAL PLUS
prodotto da
ANGELO BARBAGALLO e NANNI MORETTI
VERSIONE RESTAURATA
LA

75
Fun Flexi Flossers

LOVE
Caroline

LOCUST VALLEY
Scale 400 Feet to 1 Inch.
1906
EXPLANATORY

OPPOSITE: The family exits via the great room's side door, which leads to the original slate terrace and rear garden. The lantern is nineteenth-century English, but a new addition here.

OVERLEAF: At night, the house gives off a seductive glow and twinkles as the trees sway in the breeze, thus prompting its new moniker, *Cocuyo*, which means "firefly" in Spanish—a nod to Alfredo's Cuban heritage. The house was previously called Laurelwood, though today there are only a few laurel trees on the property. Lindeberg rarely took the easy route when it came to details, as evidenced by the varied and thoughtful brickwork on the exterior.

PAGES 258–263: The oak outdoor dining table made the move from the East Village, as did the vintage Tolix chairs, which were found at the Paris flea market.

OPPOSITE: Sebastian gets into the holiday spirit for our first Christmas in the house—a festive occasion despite the ongoing renovations (note the brown contractor's paper under his feet).

OVERLEAF: As varied as the seasons may be, the house lends itself effortlessly to the spirit of each. At holiday time, an abundance of warm Christmas lights wraps hedges and trees, keeping the festivity level high. Before moving to any new home, Alfredo has asked himself the most pressing question of all: Where will the Christmas tree go? (Given the scale of this house, the answer is . . . everywhere). On each of the three exterior sides of the primary bedroom's second-floor bay window, the zinc frame is imprinted with the delicate and detailed image of a tree—another classic Lindeberg touch.

ACKNOWLEDGMENTS

This book, as well as the many rooms, spaces, and moments featured in it, owe a giant debt of gratitude to a number of extraordinary individuals who have believed in me, nurtured me, inspired me, and worked alongside me throughout my career.

First and foremost, Ralph Lauren, who for thirty-three years gave me the creative runway to make my wildest dreams come true and who wrote the beautiful and poignant forward to this book. I am forever grateful for his mentorship, creative partnership, and extraordinary generosity—it's not unusual for employees at Ralph Lauren to stay as long or longer than I did and that says everything about Mr. Lauren as a leader. And likewise, to so many of his senior team that I had the privilege of working with during my decades at the company, specifically Buffy Birrittella, Stephen Brady, Mary Randolph Carter, Charles Fagan, Roger Farah, Francoise Labro, David Lauren, Cheryl Sterling, and the late great Jeff Walker.

At Ralph Lauren I was given the opportunity to dream big, but those big dreams would never have become reality without the support and exceptional talents of many individuals, among them Dennis Adler, Tim Albrecht, Jerry Bornkamp, Mark Cunningham, Steven Earle, Karen Elliot, Karen Ford, John Heist, John Hudson, Debra Kanabis, William Li, Donald Nowicki, Tim Pfeiffer, Quinn Pofahl, Jennifer Tsigaras, and Foster Witte. I couldn't have asked for a better or more talented group of friends and colleagues.

Our exceptional team at Alfredo Paredes Studio have continued in that same tradition, offering the vision and hard work needed to help me to realize both this project and a multitude of others, so a giant thank you to Caroline Bennett, Manrique Cartin, Claudia Levy, Bea Merry, Amelia Onishi, Jennifer Tsigaras and Marcus Tyler Van Dyke—I'm blessed to work beside all of you. And thank you to my frequent collaborators Michael Gilmore, Michelle Jacobs, John Jokinen, Michael Neumann, and Jacqueline Harrison of Harrison Green.

The creation of this book would not have been possible without the vision and expertise of the incomparable Jill Cohen and her right hand, Melissa Powell, nor to the skills and insights of editor Stacee Gravelle Lawrence. Thank you also to Charles Miers and Rizzoli for offering this project a home and sharing our work with the world—it's an honor to collaborate.

I was extremely fortunate to join forces with an array of extraordinary photographers on this project including Noe Dewitt, Miguel Flores-Viana, Douglas Friedman, Simon Upton, Isabel Parra, and Bjorn Wollander (and his assistant, Sophia Torres Pride)—the book benefitted more than I can say from each of their distinctive visions, as well as to the visual finesse of stylist, Helen Crowther. A huge thank you also to my dear friend, Richard Phibbs, for so lovingly chronicling our family over the years—we treasure your portraits. And for bringing it all together with beauty, sensitivity, and style, a huge thank you to our creative directors Doug Turshen and Steve Turner.

Lastly, the individuals in my personal life have always been key to my creative process—my siblings Loli Smith, Eddy Paredes, and Annika Varona, for partnering on some of my earliest design adventures; my parents, for allowing them to do so (and celebrating the results); and my grandmother, Maria Kindelen for supporting me in, well, just about everything. For their grounding and insightful counsel, thank you to Randy Meadoff and Sharon Kleinberg. To my children, Carolina and Sebastian, who are a constant source of inspiration and whose life-altering influence is visible on every page of this book. And finally, to my husband, Brad Goldfarb, who wrote the text for this book—thank you for always providing the lyrics to my music.

First published in the United States of America in 2025 by
Rizzoli International Publications, Inc.
49 West 27th Street
New York, NY 10001
www.rizzoliusa.com

PHOTOGRAPHY CREDITS:

Bjorn Wallander: 65, 66, 67, 72, 73, 81, 85, 87 top right, 90, 92, 93, 94-95, 96 bottom right, 99, 100-101, 111, 115, 116-117, 121, 123 bottom right, 128, 130-131, 133, 134-135, 143, 146-147, 149, 150-151, 154, 156-157, 158, 160, 161, 162,163, 164, 165, 169-181, 183, 184-185, 186, 190, 193, 196-223, 225-246, 249, 251, 252, 253, 256-257, 258-263, 268, 269

Bruce Weber: 10, courtesy of Ralph Lauren

Douglas Friedman: 68-69, 74-75, 71 top and bottom right, 76, 83, 87 bottom, 88-89

Isabel Parra: 24, 25, 38, 40, 44, 46, 48, 51, 54, 55, 56, 57, 58, 61, 63

Matthew Williams: 153

Miguel Flores Vianna: 21, 29, 31, 34-35, 37, 43, 47, 49, 50, 52-53, 60, 62

Noe DeWitt: 2-3, 6-7, 19, 166-167, 182, 187, 188, 191, 192, 194, 195, 224, 248, 254

Richard Phibbs: 82, 250

Simon Upton: 26-27, 41, 45, 96 top and bottom left, 98, 104, 105, 106-107, 110, 112, 114, 119, 125, 126, 127, 136, 137, 140, 141, 142

FINE ART CREDITS:

Page 8-9: Andrea Prandini
Page 40: Louise Bourgeois, © 2024 The Easton Foundation / Licensed by VAGA at Artists Rights Society (ARS), NY
Page 45: © Max Dupain / Copyright Agency. Licensed by Artists Rights Society (ARS), New York, 2024

Publisher: Charles Miers
Acquiring Editor: Kathleen Jayes
Project Editor: Stacee Gravelle Lawrence
Design: Doug Turshen with Steve Turner
Production Manager: Colin Hough Trapp
Managing Editor: Lynn Scrabis

Developed in collaboration with Jill Cohen Associates

ISBN: 978-0-8478-4532-3
Library of Congress Control Number: 2024946530

Printed in Hong Kong
2026 2027 2028 2029 / 10 9 8 7 6 5

Visit us online:
Instagram.com/RizzoliBooks
Facebook.com/RizzoliNewYork
Youtube.com/user/RizzoliNY

The authorized representative in the EU for product safety and compliance is Mondadori Libri S.p.A., via Gian Battista Vico 42, Milan, Italy, 20123
www.mondadori.it